first mandarin sounds

an awesome chinese word book
SIMPLIFIED CHINESE. PINYIN. ENGLISH

amanda hsiung-blodgett

Library of Congress cataloging in process
ISBN 978-1-734-7496-32

Simplified Chinese-Pinyin-English edition
Miss Panda Chinese Press

TABLE OF CONTENTS

In honor of my Father and Mother.

Thank you for giving me the gift of languages!

FOREWORD

Dear Reader,

This book is for you to help your child learn their first Mandarin sounds and words. The most effective way to introduce Mandarin sounds to the new learner is by using words. Words have meaning. Words build stories. The more children hear the accurate pronunciation of these words, the better their pronunciation becomes. Through this process we replicate the first language acquisition experience.

First Mandarin Sounds covers the thirty-seven essential sounds of Mandarin Chinese. The spoken expression of these sounds multiplies further when they are combined with Mandarin's tones. Chinese children learn these sounds assisted by the Pinyin system in mainland China, and with the Zhuyin system in Taiwan.

I make use of the Pinyin system in this book because it relies on a romanized (a, b, c...) alphabet that most non-native learners are already familiar with. This allows eager young learners to jump right in and begin the learning process without delay.

Language is for communication. See it. Listen to it. Play with it! Say it!

Let's always keep learning fun!

Amanda Hsiung-Blodgett, a.k.a. "Miss Panda"
Washington, D.C.

INTRODUCTION

How to use First Mandarin Sounds

First Mandarin Sounds is a word book that introduces the thirty-seven (37) essential sounds of the Chinese language to young learners. For each Mandarin sound introduced, the reader will also learn a high-frequency Chinese word that uses it. This allows the reader to connect the sounds with the spoken and written Chinese language, just as native learners do.

Each Mandarin sound in this book has two pages:

• First page: The featured sound, which is used within the Chinese character at the bottom of the page, is represented by its Pinyin symbol or symbols in the upper, left hand corner. These Pinyin symbols are also hidden inside the picture once for the reader to find.

On this page, the reader should look at and pronounce the pinyin symbol, then find it within the picture, and finally study the Chinese character. Use the Pinyin pronunciation chart provided at the back of this book, as needed, for assistance with how to express the sounds of these Pinyin characters.

• Second page: On this page the full Pinyin pronunciation of the featured word is written at the bottom with an English translation provided below it. The reader should use the Pinyin provided to say the word aloud.

This page is also designed with a playful, "look & find" style, as readers can practice the sound and word containing it by locating the three sets of the Chinese character or characters hidden within the picture, or randomly located on the page.

Have fun!

Glossary

Includes the complete list of Chinese words used in *First Mandarin Sounds*. There are also fifteen (15) common Chinese sentence patterns that parents can use to interact and engage young readers. Each item is written out in Chinese, Pinyin, and English.

Pronunciation Chart

A chart in English, Pinyin, and Zhuyin is provided. Pinyin, a system that uses romanization (A, B, C, et cetera) to approximate the sounds of Chinese characters/words, is widely used in Mainland Chinese. Zhuyin, a system that makes use of thirty-seven unique symbols to capture the essential sounds of Mandarin Chinese, is mainly used in Taiwan.

Bonuses

You can visit MissPandaChinese.com to claim your exclusive bonus video and related playsheets.

first
mandarin
sounds

b

爸爸

bà ba
dad

p

婆婆

pó po
Grandmother (mom's mom)

m

马

mǎ
horse

f

飞机

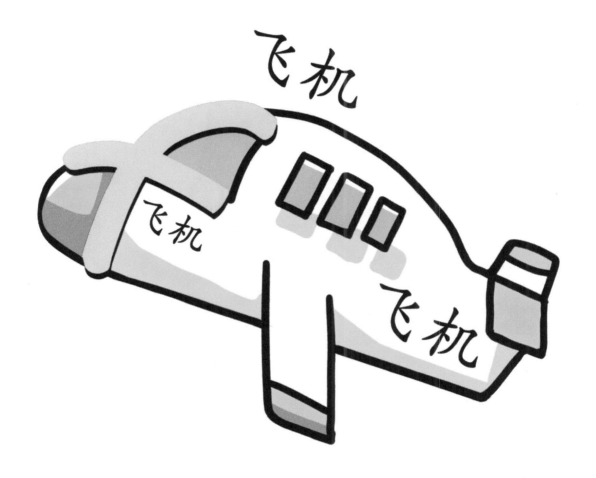

fēi jī
airplane

d

弟弟

dì di
younger brother

兔子

兔子

兔子

兔子

tù zi
rabbit

n

鸟

niǎo

bird

篮球

篮球

lán qiú
basketball

g

哥哥

哥哥

gē ge
older brother

k

蝌蚪

kē dǒu

tadpole

h

蝴蝶

hú dié
butterfly

j

鸡

jī
chicken

q

球

qiú
ball

X

西瓜

xī guā
watermelon

zh

猪

zhū

pig

ch

车

chē

car

sh

书

shū
book

r

人

人

rén
person

紫色

zǐ sè
Purple (color)

C

草莓

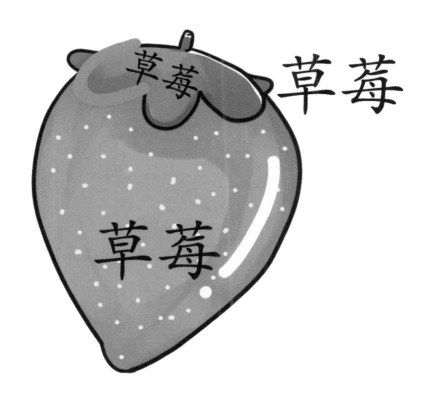

căo méi
strawberry

S

sǎn

umbrella

衣服

yī fú
clothes

u

乌龟

wū guī
turtle

ü

鱼

yú

fish

a

阿姨

ā yí

aunt

O

火山

huǒ shān

volcano

e

鹅

é

goose

ye

爷爷

爷爷

yé ye
Grandfather (dad's dad)

ai

爱

ài
love

ei

黑色

黑色 黑色

黑色 黑色

hēi sè

black

ao

猫

māo
cat

ou

手

shǒu

hand

an

安静

安静

安静

安静

ān jìng

silence

en

蚊子

wén zi
mosquito

ang

王子

wáng zǐ

prince

eng

风

fēng

wind

er

耳朵

耳朵

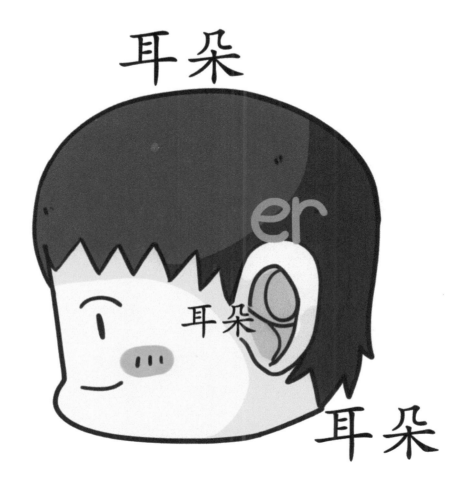

耳朵

耳朵

ěr duo

ear

First Mandarin Sounds & Words
Glossary

English	Simplified Chinese	Pinyin
airplane	飞机	fēi jī
aunt	阿姨	ā yí
ball	球	qiú
basketball	篮球	lán qiú
bird	鸟	niǎo
black (color)	黑色	hēi sè
book	书	shū
butterfly	蝴蝶	hú dié
car	车	chē
cat	猫	māo
chicken	鸡	jī
clothing	衣服	yī fú
dad	爸爸	bà ba

First Mandarin Sounds & Words
Glossary

English	Simplified Chinese	Pinyin
ear	耳朵	ěr duo
fish	鱼	yú
goose	鹅	é
grandfather (dad's side)	爷爷	yé ye
grandmother (dad's side)	婆婆	pó po
hand	手	shǒu
horse	马	mǎ
love	爱	ài
mosquito	蚊子	wén zi
older brother	哥哥	gē ge
person	人	rén
pig	猪	zhū
prince	王子	wáng zi

First Mandarin Sounds & Words
Glossary

English	Simplified Chinese	Pinyin
purple (color)	紫色	zǐ sè
quiet	安静	ān jìng
rabbit	兔子	tù zi
strawberry	草莓	cǎo méi
tadpole	蝌蚪	kē dǒu
turtle	乌龟	wū guī
umbrella	伞	sǎn
volcano	火山	huǒ shān
watermelon	西瓜	xī guā
wind	风	fēng
younger brother	弟弟	dì di
What is this?	这是什么？	Zhè shì shén me?
This is...	这是…	Zhè shì…。

First Mandarin Sounds & Words
Glossary

English	Simplified Chinese	Pinyin
Is this…?	这是···吗?	Zhè shì… ma?
Yes. | No.	是。| 不是。	Shì。| Bú shì。
I (don't) know.	我(不)知道。	Wǒ (bù) zhī dào.
Do you have…?	你有···吗?	Nǐ yǒu…ma?
I have…	我有···。	Wǒ yǒu…。
I don't have…	我沒有···。	Wǒ méi yǒu…。
Do you like…?	你喜欢... 吗?	Nǐ xǐ huān…ma?
I like…	我喜欢···。	Wǒ xǐ huān…。
I don't like…	我不喜欢···。	Wǒ bù xǐ huān…。
Do you see…?	你看到···吗?	Nǐ kàn dào…ma?
I see…	我看到···。	Wǒ kàn dào…。
Where is it?	在哪里?	Zài nǎ lǐ?
It's here!	在这里!	Zài zhè lǐ!

First Mandarin Sounds
Mandarin Chinese Pronunciation Chart

PINYIN	ENGLISH	ZHUYIN
b	**b**ook	ㄅ
p	**p**ay	ㄆ
m	**m**om	ㄇ
f	**f**irst	ㄈ
d	**d**uck	ㄉ
t	**t**ea	ㄊ
n	**n**oon	ㄋ
l	**l**oud	ㄌ
g	**g**ood	ㄍ
k	**k**ick	ㄎ
h	**h**ot	ㄏ
j	**jee**p	ㄐ
q	**chee**tos	ㄑ
x	**shee**t	ㄒ
zh	gara**ge**	ㄓ
ch	**ch**urch	ㄔ
sh	**sh**irt	ㄕ
r	**r**ose	ㄖ
z	ro**ds**	ㄗ

First Mandarin Sounds
Mandarin Chinese Pronunciation Chart

PINYIN	ENGLISH	ZHUYIN
c	wha**t's**	ㄘ
s	**s**it	ㄙ
i / yi/ -i	b**ee**	ㄧ
U / wu/ -u	b**oo**	ㄨ
ü / yu/ lü/ nü/-u	f**ue**l	ㄩ
a	**a**-ha	ㄚ
o	**oh**	ㄛ
e	m**a**chine	ㄜ
-e	ye	y**e**t	ㄝ
ai	**I**	ㄞ
ei	h**ey**	ㄟ
ao	**ou**ch	ㄠ
ou	**aw**ful	ㄡ
an	t**an**	ㄢ
en	n**un**	ㄣ
ang	p**on**d	ㄤ
eng	l**ung**	ㄥ
er	b**ir**d	ㄦ

High-Frequency Words You Can Use with First Mandarin Sounds

Family & Friends

爸 爸	妈 妈	哥 哥	姊 姊	弟 弟	妹 妹
bà ba	mā ma	gē ge	jiě jie	dì di	mèi mei
dad	mom	older brother	older sister	younger brother	younger sister

公 公	婆 婆	爷 爷	奶 奶	阿 姨	叔 叔
gōng gong	pó po	yé ye	nǎi nai	ā yí	shū shu
grandpa (mom's side)	grandma (mom's side)	grandpa (dad's side)	grandma (dad's side)	aunt (in general & mom's sister)	uncle (in general & dad's brother)

老 师	同 学	朋 友	家 人	我	你
lǎo shī	tóng xué	péng yǒu	jiā rén	wǒ	nǐ
teacher	classmate	friend	family member	I, me	you

他 （她）	我 们	你 们	他 们	大 家	宠 物
tā	wǒ men	nǐ men	tā men	dà jiā	chǒng wù
he, him (she, her)	we, us	you,	they, them	everyone	pet

Power Words

有	没 有	是	不 是	要	不 要
yǒu	méi yǒu	shì	bú shì	yào	bú yào
has, have there is/are	don't have there is/are not	yes	no	want	don't want

喜 欢	不 喜 欢	吃	不 吃	知 道	不 知 道
xǐ huān	bù xǐ huān	chī	bù chī	zhī dào	bù zhī dào
like	don't like	eat	don't eat	know	don't know

ACKNOWLEDGEMENTS

Thank You to my husband for his unwavering support. Thank You to my children for their continuing inspiration.

Sincere "Thank Yous" also to the following:

My dear Sparkables: Donna Kirsh, Randah Taher, Staci Boden, Julia Mines, Haile McCollum, and Mary Elizabeth Sheehan.

My fellow Chinese language and culture teacher friends: Pamela Rose, Lea Ekeberg, Trudy Owens, and La Sripanawongsa.

Two amazing artists: my illustrator from Taiwan, Wang Yu-Wen; and my cover designer, Sue Hoffmeyer of s j z design in Washington, D.C.

ABOUT THE AUTHOR

Amanda Hsiung-Blodgett is an experienced language educator, the creator of "Miss Panda Chinese," a popular online resource for parents and educators, and the host of the *Playful Chinese* podcast. She has taught ESL and Chinese language to non-native speakers on four continents.

Amanda is the Chinese language consultant for The Jim Henson Company's *Word Party* Season 4 on Netflix. She was a former executive at Warner Bros. and has served as a professional interpreter for Hollywood celebrities and such famous personalities as motivational speaker Tony Robbins, as well as numerous Fortune 500 companies.

Amanda was also the co-host for the *English Club*, the top-rated English language learning program on the National Education Radio Station in Taiwan, the radio equivalent of PBS in the United States.

Amanda Hsiung-Blodgett